Wet Underbelly Wind

poems by

Nicole Farmer

Finishing Line Press
Georgetown, Kentucky

Wet Underbelly Wind

Copyright © 2022 by Nicole Farmer
ISBN 979-8-88838-054-3 First Edition
All rights reserved under International and Pan-American Copyright Conventions. No part of this book may be reproduced in any manner whatsoever without written permission from the publisher, except in the case of brief quotations embodied in critical articles and reviews.

ACKNOWLEDGMENTS

Thank you to the editors and readers of the following journals in which the following poems were first published, sometimes in an earlier version, either online or in print:

Atlantis Creative Magazine: "Survivants"
Bangalore Review: "Homesick for the Dead"
Change Seven: "83"(Sonnet 83)
Closed Eye Open: "The sound and smell of rain in the night"
Day Eight (Bourgeon Magazine): "Dead Man's Toenails", "No Going Back" (I remember the doughnuts)
East By Northeast Literary Review: "Dance of Death", "Mother's Day"
Great Smokies Review: "visiting my child who has become an adult"
Haunted Waters Press: "Daughter and Mother"
Quillkeepers Press: "The Secret"
Kakalak Review: "Dyslexia"
Road Runner Review: "Role Reversal"
Tiny Seed Literary Journal: "wild"
You Might Need to Hear This: "The Secret"
Viewless Wings Literary Magazine: "why the girl?"

Publisher: Leah Huete de Maines
Editor: Christen Kincaid
Cover Art: Nicole Farmer
Author Photo: Nicole Farmer
Cover Design: Elizabeth Maines McCleavy

Order online: www.finishinglinepress.com
also available on amazon.com

Author inquiries and mail orders:
Finishing Line Press
PO Box 1626
Georgetown, Kentucky 40324
USA

Table of Contents

Wanting More 1

No Going Back 2

Time 3

Nineteen 4

dyslexia c. 1972 5

visiting my child who has become an adult 6

wild 7

Daughter and Mother 8

Shibui List 9

homesick for the dead 10

Role Reversal 11

Rescue 12

Survivants 13

Dead Man's Toenails 14

The Secret 15

26 in 2020 16

Why the girl? 17

Dance of Death 18

You 19

Mother's Day 20

The Shit We Don't Know 21

the sound and smell of rain in the night 22

83 23

Longing 24

shoulda, woulda, coulda 25

*As if to look down
on the dead is to look up
at my own face, trampled
by music.*
—Ocean Vuong

*For Loren and Donna, who inspired.
For Sally and Minx, my muses.*

Wanting More

I kneel on the grass in this swampy Louisiana yard,
where my father once buried his mother's ashes
and crowned them with a red rose bush,
nestled against the bricks of his melting house.
My father just died in the bedroom behind this wall,
where we have flung all the windows wide
to let his spirit soar, as if it could
be contained, and something called me to seek
a flower in all this oppressive heat,
and one of Amelia's roses has survived the onslaught.
I will touch his waxen eyelids one at a time
to place a single petal upon them just as the Aztecs did.
How simple and childish to feel so robbed.
The tips of his fingers sound like the moans
of cows lowing to their missing calves in the field below
where my heart lies bruised as a fallen peach.

No Going Back

I can never go back there; I know this is true because I visited the old neighborhood just last July and it's simply gone, a ghost not a community, filled with condemned shot-gun shacks, broken sidewalks, dirt for lawns, and condemned signs. The old 7-11 is a building that lies gutted with a sign in the fractured window that reads *Easy Taxes 1-2-3*. When I was a kid, I emptied the coin jar early on Sunday mornings and walked three blocks in the throbbing heat to buy a dozen day-old doughnuts from Daffy's on the corner, for 79 cents. When I returned dad would have chicory coffee brewing and my sister would have sliced an orange or apple to share. We three sat on the back deck under the giant pecan tree grinning like fools. This is the life! I remember thinking. To this day I can't eat a fresh hot doughnut—it just tastes wrong.

Time

I've seen the face of humanity
and it wasn't etched on the pyramid wall,

but in the exquisite nose of the Mayan
who sold me a wooden mask
of the exact same profile.

Our story doesn't die
with the fall of empires—
it lives in the toenails of the unborn,

and the butterfly who knows the secret,
as she alights on the Kapok tree,
and in its leaves that blow in the wind
even as a branch crumbles and decays below
reminding us that

tombs don't restrain the dead.

Nineteen

She's nineteen, naughty, nimble, a jumble of nerves and curves,
taking all she obviously deserves from the endless
dripping-hot south, cicadas pounding, "summer, summer,
breed, breed". He's in her play, her romance, her solo spectacular
splash into Tennessee Williams and sweet sin. She bends
and reaches for a kiwi. Furry round mystery rolling around
in her ravenous hands. *Cut it. Cut it up*, he grins. She laughs
a gurgling laugh, throws back her head, so he sees all her teeth,
then whispers, "Let's peel it, feel it wet in our fingers
until we mash it between our faces".
Mouths still dripping, they're flying
down the stairs, racing to the convertible of their wanton,
willing surrender, desire sloshing in their tight tan bellies,
to drive fast, into the salacious seduction of the twilight.

dyslexia c. 1972

teacher at the bord standing, row center starts with paragraf one them, and i'm counting and sweeting memorise my paragraphe without turn, i'm squirming, hart beating in front of me ascs to go to the falling down into darkness, unable failure, and the resounding silense DUNCE cap placed on my

social studies book in hand, first kid, first then the next kid back, then the next behind dreding reading and re-reading, trying to any flaws, it's getting closr and closer to my too fast, trying to breathe, when the kid bathroom, and i'm falling, falling, to see or heer anything except my own of turned heds, gawking to see the enormus head

visiting my child who has become an adult

no hot food or fresh cut flowers await me, just the warmth of your flesh and your sleepy smile and all the corona virus rules we broke to indulge in this moment like no other with my nose in your hair and that familiar smell of the perfume only your head can make and my heart misses a beat and the world stands still from its constant spinning and I am content to be wherever you are standing in the marijuana haze drifting out the door of your apartment which I know must be yours because of the moldy croissants in a plastic box you hastily tossed in your frantic cleaning to show me the beauty of the home you have made and decorated with care for you and your sweetie—but all I can do is look at your long delicate fingers, each like a butterfly wing, as you gesture for me to step inside.

wild

in the forest i turn feral, grow matted thick red fur, feel my nose extend to a spear point. in the forest i hunt animals with alarming speed and no fear, my teeth and claws sharp and merciless, i have lightning speed and strength. in the forest i have no babes to suckle or save, i am no one's mother. in the forest i am a killer, feared and respected. i am invisible in the dark except for the green glow of my eyes. in the forest man has never touched me. in the forest the underbrush is thick and dense and seeing the sky is rare, i smell everything that has gone before and everything that hides, i have no thought of the future only the moment. in the forest i am content in my aloneness, unhindered by a mate or offspring, i tread on pine needles, crunching leaves, moss, mushrooms, and seeds from scat, knowing exactly the direction of my den. in the forest i am untethered, unattached, fierce and god like.

Daughter and Mother

She calls me from the road.
I sit on a stool in my little blue kitchen.
She tells me she knows how to change a tire now.
I eat cottage cheese and marvel.
She pitched a tent near Carlsbad Caverns, cooked baked beans.
I planted seventeen tomato plants in holes I cut in the black plastic garden patch.
She went to Joshua tree and dug a sand-stuck car out of the desert with two ice scrapers.
I cooked spaghetti sauce with tomatoes, fresh basil, garlic, and artichoke hearts.
She slept in a deserted cabin infested with rats, which she ran screaming from at four am.
I sit at my desk and stare at the blank page, waiting for a muse to descend.
She marches in the pro-Palestine demonstration in Los Angeles.
I make lists of art supplies for my summer camp.
She jogs on the beach in Venice.
I walk laps at the high school track.
She blind dates a Nordic Amazon in Long Beach, but no sparks fly.
I laugh at her stories and smack my knee.
She is a phoenix rising each morning with her wounded heart dripping blood down to her knees, beams of sunshine streaming out of her eye sockets.
I await her next call, like a chapter in a suspense novel.
She weaves a story better than any spider does her web and her laughter makes my head bubble and fizz like exploding joy from a champagne bottle.
She is cast from fire.
I am spun from water.

Shibui List

Saying no.

Not caring when you laugh too long or clap too loud.

Realizing you're just as fabulous in Keds as stilettos.

Appreciating your friends and their ability to make you smile.

Knowing you look better without make-up, but never giving up lipstick!

Being just as happy with a quiet day in the garden and reading good book, as you would with dinner and a show.

Taking nothing for granted.

Welcoming the idea of no longer being valued for your sex appeal alone.

Feeling weaker of body and stronger of mind.

Having a good chuckle over failure, instead of a crying jag.

Smiling when others cut you off in traffic.

Looking forward to your morning cup of tea.

Noticing tree blossoms.

Smelling the rain.

Enjoying the success of your children more than you enjoy your own.

The beauty of aging.

homesick for the dead

Stumbling through the dust of cremation bones, I dream of rivers rolling wide and green and deep—time is an abstraction—you walk beside me in rhythm from another age, our words carried on the wet wind to the underworld. My life is as small and tenuous as a drop of dew suspended in a spider's web. A dragonfly lives only four months when lucky; we shake our heads at the shortness of their lives, just as the stars pity us our brief, human days on Earth. What good is my next breath without you? I want to roll down the muddy Mississippi to the ocean, suspended in the cool bubbles churned under a sternwheeler, my existence no more significant than a raindrop, sorrow drifting like perfume from a magnolia flower, as your laughter rings in my head and the melody from the neighborhood ice cream truck fades steadily down the block.

Role Reversal

My oldest daughter instructs me on how to behave after my first vaccination.
I consult her when making travel decisions.
She is twenty-six.
I am fifty-eight.
She talks to me in a tone of patient understanding.
I want to tell her what a wild child I was in my twenties.
She expounds on Democracy Now.
I want her to read Dickens, to laugh.
She tells me to call her back so we can discuss the Middle East.
I promise to read the book she has given me on the nature of relationships.
She dreams of women being raped and being unable to help them.
I dream of jumping so high that my head pops above pink clouds.
Her middle name should be Caution, not Rose.
I have no middle name, but I think I would like Contenta.
She is the virus expert.
I am an aging hippie chick.
Her anger lights the room on fire.
My feet wander outdoors with no shoes.

Rescue

Screen door slams, a flash of red
in the road as I approach—
a giant crow swoops in with a strategic peck
at the neck. I am running, arms flailing, seeing
one red wing bent, but not severed, pointing
at the heavens like an accusing finger, then
a passing car almost mashes him flat.

No movement. I fetch a dishtowel
dash to scoop him up—he squawks in protest,
alive and fighting. Setting him gently
among some bluebells, I see
the crow circling for another divebomb attempt.
I scream and charge him.
He perches on a branch to outwait me.
As I whisper words of love to my stunned cardinal,

I flash on the time you rescued me
from a Louisiana jail cell after eight hours
of waiting, my one phone call made
to Grandma Amelia, only to hear her pause,
then say, *I'll tell your father*, CLICK, making it clear
she sure as hell wasn't coming.
Caught shoplifting, terrified—
when I heard your voice echo
down the long corridor the fluttering
in my stomach stilled. Though I did not know,
at sixteen, you had done time.
My love for you that day changed
in a way we never had to discuss.

The cardinal just hopped up and
looked around at the bright blue sky.

Survivants

Three women padding barefoot
around the wood floors of a cheery home
amidst the flat mud green
wasteland of Louisiana lawns.
Three generations,
mother, daughter, and grandmother split
open wide with grief
and joy—finding comfort
in each other's laughter during this
forbidden coronavirus visit.

Floating through ancient Cypress trees
whose knobby knees kiss
a blue crack of sky, through winking
Spanish moss eyelashes—
our drifting boat rocks, daring
sleepy-eyed alligators to perform their favorite trick.
Displaced French tourists seek lunch conversation
screeching vacation RV wheels spin,
stuck in the swamp
mud, crunching apples, salty olives
mud, New Yorker crossword puzzle,
peanut butter and marmalade sighs.

A mockingbird pitches his song in oak
branches scratching puffy drifting clouds,
wet underbelly wind caressing my neck—
the patriarch now gone,
whispers of churning discontent
in sublime contentment.

Dead Man's Toenails

Every time I look down, there he is—
thick disease-ridden hooves for nails,
dad's gift to me, which I've resented
my entire life.

Briefly the blame fell on walking barefoot
in cow manure as a kid, that was my mother's guess.
Now I realize it's my inheritance
this hideous prize; a reminder of
the old man's genetic magic.

Every time I clip, file and polish
these yellow crustaceans of crumbling decay
my only wish is to vanish this curse.

If I could resurrect the dead,
I'd dance a two-step with my dad
on our peasant feet!

THE SECRET

Blue
The sky weeps big pelting drops on the window. Outside the brown leaps from the trees in a windswept blur. Here, inside, my mother reaches for my hand by feeling around on the bed covers as if she is blind. She cries out for me. The death grip pulls her hard, so she clings to my warmth with a Herculean strength. Her voice like a crocodile hiss. *I have something to tell you I have never told anyone before.* Intake of breath as I fall forward into the cerulean unknown.

Green
Her eyes so pale and deep-set like a field of new clover darkened by shadows, now red-rimmed and puffy. Tired of it all. She tells me she had *five* daughters—two she gave away, and I hear her dementia laughing at me. Hospital walls of puke green tighten around us, and I try to correct her. *No Mom, It's just me and my sis, and the unwanted pregnancy before marriage.* She has no patience for my interruption— the story unfolds like an artichoke heart revealing it's thorn.

Purple
Two, she says, created for a couple who couldn't have kids. She, the ripe plumb, impregnated with a turkey baster from the fertile dad, not my dad, long before the term surrogate even existed. Not twins. Twice she did this. For them. For my dad—to put him through graduate school. Not for herself, never for herself. Behind my left ear I hear something pop. Blood placenta five times generated.

Orange
I hide in the sanctuary of my car. The hurricane rages around me—sheets of rain littering my windshield with leaves of rust, ginger, tiger and fire. While she sleeps, I drive mindlessly down dead-end streets decorated with grinning Halloween pumpkins. Can this be true? When I said, *Oh Mom, that must have been so hard for you*, she said, *No, no it was easy really*, in that dreamy, distant way she looks right through you into a world you will never know. She turned her head away and curled into a coiled oleander caterpillar.

Yellow
Stumbling around the aisles of Target in a daze with sunshine colored Pine Sol in my cart—I don't remember how I got here. Who can I call? Dad died six months ago. My sister is in China and it's 3 am in Tianjin. Somewhere on this planet are two slightly older women, my half-sisters, walking around with no knowledge that their genetic mother is dying. I push my cart into the sock isle and pick out bright lemon booties for mom's tiny bird-boned feet. Parts of me, parts of you, amber tone seagull bones.

White
The sky has melted and is running down my pale face, in mascara streams till my tears no longer taste of salt. All the Goth girls want the number of my stylist. I reverse out of the parking space, and almost run over an old man with a walker—I scream like a punctured tire and pound the steering wheel. I close my eyes and all I see is a blistering white starburst of rage. Why didn't she tell me sooner? Will I find the courage to ask her more? Stepping into the rehabilitation center, disinfectant mixed with feces hits my nose, and the floor quicksands under my feet. I am sinking into a milky abyss.

Black
Hurtling into the great unknown, sucked into a black hole where the truth I knew has disappeared—mom sleeps. With this new knowledge, thinking of my parents' marriage, the odd comments—*That Donna, you look at her sideways and she's pregnant!* —is like the distortion of a fun house mirror. Small town factory girl who ran away to the Big Apple, became a successful model, only to give it all up to support her man. No one to question about her dark undisclosed act of martyrdom. My scorched heart shrivels like a raisin. Three more hours and I can call my sister. Three days later she is gone. She dies alone, just as she said she would. In my blackest midnight, she sailed away, with no further words for me.

26 in 2020

Oh, you intense and angry one, my first born, so displaced so displeased and uprooted in an upside-down year where you lost your job, apartment, and a boyfriend you deeply loved: living out of your car and couch-surfing in the homes of friends and family, you of the vivid dreams about the end of the world, terrorized by the coronavirus, and adamant that "T*here is NO back to normal!* You whose eyes flash with fire and widen to popping, as you talk about the evils of capitalism and the importance of community, you whose laugh is an explosion of joy at a Tweet about the ironies of love, who cries every time you watch *It's a Wonderful Life*, and cries again while you talk with your online therapist, you who jump up and applaud with a hoot on hearing that Bernie is going to filibuster on the floor of the senate. As your shirt rides up, I see the scars from the blows you took along your arm and ribs from some riot-control police officer in Chicago, who must have forgotten how much he loves his own daughter.

Why the girl?

I'm so sorry, comes out of my mouth, and I know the words do not suffice. What should I have said? My new friend has just told me his daughter was a free spirit, how he is writing songs about her for the first time. He says she was murdered five years ago. How to describe the rest of my evening? I cried in my car the whole way home, imagining the mysterious undeserved death of an untamable girl just turned twenty. With no details except, *she got herself in a bad situation*, my mind races. Why is it always the girl? Girls die at the hands of a man hundreds of times a day, for hundreds of reasons: he wanted her body, he was ashamed of her body, he was ashamed for wanting her body, he wanted her money, he resented her money, he had to punish her and take her money, he hated her freedom, he was threatened by her freedom, he wanted her freedom, he took her freedom to feel better about resenting her freedom, she was in his way, she should pay for being in his way, he was attracted to her and it was her fault, he had to rape her and kill her in order to feel better about the fact that he resented her, he had to rape her because he could not control himself, and that was her fault, so she deserved to die, this girl—any girl—who is simply there, and inconvenient to his agenda. What to say? I can only hold his hand and listen, if he should ever want to speak again about the father he once was.

Dance of Death

In this dance I sashay the track,
awash with squiggling earthworms after
the heavy rains and unseasonably warm night. I sidestep,
trying not to land and squash, like a giant
Norse god picking his way through a battlefield strewn
with bodies both dead and living, I hop over and
miss these inching, writhing forms so far below me,
to save a life, then ponder, when squished will they not
split and go their separate ways?

Why are the birds not descending?

Are their bellies sufficiently gorged on the morning's feast?

Exercise is an obstacle course—
unlike the Cyclops I carry on a single minded
quest of mercy.

Some stars live millions of years, some people
make one hundred, worms less than six—

                              none of us more than a blink of an eye.

YOU

I hear your voice on the other end of
the line and my mind celebrates with trumpets.

Just those two small words, *Hi Mom*,
and my heart beats stronger

the surprise lightens
the timber of my voice

because you are calling me, yes ME
and I didn't even ask you to.

Your simple gesture is enough
to change my day,

as a party starts in my stomach,
like dancing jellybeans

about to be spilled
from a swinging pinata

whose prizes are still hidden,
still a mystery.

Mother's Day

This day and every day until my end of days, I have
nothing but time to remember, to celebrate everything

about you I hold dear, with a burning longing
and memories that don't fade, like a cactus misses the rain.

You, snapping your fingers and stomping your feet
at the first note blasting from the stereo.

You, offering me a piece of Trident gum like it were
a depression child's secret dream, a twinkle in your eyes.

You, walking six blocks in the pouring rain and wind
just to see my new haircut and clap your hands in glee.

You, making me smell your breath before you step out
the front door, blowing minty wind in my face to be sure.

You, with my head in your lap, stroking my hair methodically,
rubbing my back so I dare not move, or even breathe.

The Shit We Don't Know

Call it the dirt swept under the carpet
Call it the miracle of stardust stuck in the marrow of your bones
Call it the secrets your parents kept from you

Whatever you name it, there is simply so much unknown in this life:

Your mother telling you she had two daughters she gave away
(whispered on her deathbed)
Your father's days turned into months in solitary confinement
(a natural storyteller mute on this subject)
A perennial plant turns green again in the spring
(a resurrection uncelebrated)

And truth?
What is truth?

It's the web a front porch spider spins each night, fresh with the dew
It's the dreams that do not vanish after we wake to a new dawn
It's the small death we experience every time we hiccup

I am infantile in my ignorance,
childlike in my wonder.

the sound and smell of rain in the night

window open, as I need it to slumber
i am awoken from my dreams by the reassuring

sound of water drizzling, dripping, draining
pelting sheets of nourishing encouragement,

the sigh of sustenance, life force, pitter patter.
with ease of mind, I snuggle down under

my covers and smile, nothing can go wrong now
with that quenching quiver of relief

and earth smells of fungus, mold, mildew, decay—
new life all rolled into one. from the

desolate darkness comes light and growth.
sleep is deepened, dreams dance in my heavy

cranium, mirth and magic materialize
in this nurturing prize, all is well, and the spell is cast

for continuum, life, lavish and long—but wait
this is day five of the deluge and isn't there a

flood warning?

83

I can see them so clearly, those tiny perfect feet
slender with high arches and toes that gripped the earth
in some strange miracle of double-jointed wonder—
crinkle toes I called them—the feet I adored,
coveted, pedestal to the beautiful, enigmatic
daydreamer of a doe, my mother. Still the proud
owner of those magical hooves made for dancing
now head in the clouds dementia that travels down to
her base, causing an unstable wobble of delicate
bones and muscle that are shrinking, drying, crumbling
daily. Still this eighty-one-pound dynamo marches
down the street with rapid fire forward motion, arms
akimbo, weaving like a noon-day drunk, whistling like
a sailor and winking at me as if she knows the secret.

Longing

I say love is the aroma of lavender,
        because herbs are the closest I can get to your smell.

I say language is yearning and words fall short,
        because missing you leaves me tongue-tied.

I say god is a mouth full of spaghetti sauce,
        because tasting is the way I can hear your laughter again.

I say meaning is the photographs I ogle,
        because images quell the fear of forgetting you.

I say living is remembering a kaleidoscope of moments,
        because reliving them gives me courage to face the unknown.

I say survival is blood in the veins of my family,
        because kinship is what sustains me in the darkness.

shoulda, woulda, coulda

I should be writing a short story
I could be cleaning the house,

but all I want to do this lazy, sunny,
unexpectedly warm November afternoon

is read and nap on the back deck with my best pal,
the squirrel slayer, a fifteen-pound terrier.

Sunlight makes bright orange splotches
behind my closed eye lids, the warmth melts my muscles,

like maple syrup on buttered pancakes.
Who can work under these conditions, really!?

Leaf musk from the rustling creek drifts to me,
a woodpecker's pleasant pecking far across the field—

these are the dog days we wish for, when
winter's howling winds keeps us inside.

I will follow my canine's lead—stretch,
yawn and roll over, toward the last rays of the day.

Personal Thanks

I wish to give a special thanks to my husband and first reader, Mark, my editor, April Ossmann, and to all my teachers at The Great Smokies Writing Program who have been instrumental in keeping me writing and rewriting. My love to my sister, Carrie, for her ongoing support, and to my stepmother, Virginia, for her encouragement.

Nicole Farmer is a writer and reading tutor. She is a graduate of the Juilliard School of Drama. Her poetry has appeared in a variety of print and online publications, including *The Closed Eye Open, Quillkeepers Press, Capsule Stories, Sheepshead Review, Roadrunner Review, Wild Roof Journal, Bacopa Literary Review, Great Smokies Review, Kakalak Review, 86 Logic, Wingless Dreamer, Inlandia Review, In Parentheses*, and many others. She was awarded the First Prize in Prose Poetry from the *Bacopa Literary Review* in 2020. She currently resides in Asheville, NC with her husband and their grumpy Carin terrier. You can find her dancing barefoot in her driveway on the full moon at midnight.

www.ingramcontent.com/pod-product-compliance
Lightning Source LLC
Chambersburg PA
CBHW022127090426
42743CB00008B/1036